Carry Your Shoes and Come

Michael Lewis Owen

Editor	**Ann Tegwen Hughes**
Illustrator	**Gerallt Hughes**
ICT Formatting	**James LC Owen**
Trinity Trilogy Chant	**Chris Roberts**

Contents

Editor's Preface

How many times does good come from bad, I wonder? Happily, most myths, legends, stories and folk tales tell us that this is usually the case; usually, remember, not always. At this very moment you are holding another, newer example and I certainly hope you'll take off your shoes, sit down in comfort, relax and read on.

Carry Your Shoes and Come has been produced for several reasons. Michael Lewis Owen wrote these poems during periods of reflection, prayer and devotion, at a time, when each and everyone of us needed reassurance, support and guidance. Though you may argue that these three things are always necessary, in 2020, our whole world was affected by an unforeseen, invisible force; we need no reminders of how it has changed us all (and it shall not have the satisfaction of being named)!

Michael channelled his feelings, prayed and wrote on a daily basis, after all, he had the time, didn't we all? Although he would argue that the guidance he received was God-given and the words produced were a gift from the Holy Spirit; the resulting poems, all so relevant to our lives today, came from his vision. The vast breadth of this volume's subject matter is quite intriguing, as it moves from tales of people who lived on this earth a long, long time ago, to stories we know about the birth of Jesus, leading to so many wondrous happenings in a short span of around thirty years.

Over these past strange years, we have all realised how often we need someone in our lives. There is guidance and hope here in this book. The final sections suggest ways of being mindful, of using prayer and meditation, of heeding warnings, but ultimately, greeting the sun into our lives. It shows us ways of treading paths carefully, however rough or smooth, wide or narrow they may be, so that we may improve our own lives and those of others too.

Intended for anyone needing reassurance for any reason, Michael also wanted so much to ensure that *Carry Your Shoes and Come* might be sold to support and recognize the dedicated, wonderful, constant work carried out by those at Tŷ Gobaith in Conwy and Hope House, Oswestry. The love, respect, care and attention each one receives there as patient, parent, relative, friend or visitor; the work carried out through therapy, counselling, supporting of family members during times of need, loss, hopelessness and desolation is immeasurable. YOU make light out of darkness; thank-you. Diolch i bawb yn Nhŷ Gobaith. So do, please consider using the QR code at the back of this book to engage further in the development and growth of this wonderful haven for children, young people, and their families.

I would suggest that many of us could benefit from owning a copy of *Carry Your Shoes and Come*! Not only will you be supporting Tŷ Gobaith, this amazing charity, but you will also benefit from reading Michael's words. Dip in, read a little, read a lot. This book would certainly be a very useful resource and companion for teachers, at school or Sunday School and for anyone who is uncertain of whom Susanna, Daniel and Darius were, what happened to the Spendthrift

Son and why on earth people were on one occasion, able to hear: '*An orchestra in different tongues.*' A copy would be invaluable too in places of worship. Michael has ensured that there are full Biblical references at the end of the book.

You will find an elegant symbol dotted around the pages and relevant musical suggestions available on YouTube; obviously, you will also choose your very own favourite melodies to complement the poems! A chant to reflect the unity of the Trinity, has kindly been written by Chris Roberts, composer and Director of Music at St Mary's, Conwy.

So, dear friends, kick off those shoes, please, and get reading!

With love, gyda chariad, Ann.

Ann Tegwen Hughes

Joyful Collaboration: It has been a profound privilege to work in harmony and co-operate together on this project. Michael a convinced Catholic; Chris a dynamic member of the Church in Wales and Ann an enthusiastic member of a Welsh Presbyterian Chapel, we like to think of ourselves here as offering a small example of Christian Unity in action.

Acknowledgements

I would first like to thank my wife Sue who looked over these pieces as they were written, asked probing questions and ironed out many errors. This meant that when I handed a booklet of the poems to Ann Tegwen Hughes they were at least presentable. Ann has proved a brilliant editor. She suggested the overall framework. She has also edited each poem very carefully and suggested numerous improvements. Indeed, whilst being guided by Ann, I have glimpsed how fortunate her university students must have been as she prepared them for entering the teaching profession. She has also suggested some music that readers might like to access as they read this book. She plays the piano, sings in a number of choirs and has a love of music like so many do in this land of song. I would also like to thank Gerallt Hughes and James Owen for giving their skill and time so generously to this venture where all royalties are going to Tŷ Gobaith to support its work of helping sick children and their families. It was wonderful for Ann and me to find Andy Everley, of Tŷ Gobaith Conwy, and his colleagues so welcoming and open to the idea of this book. Finally I would like to thank my friend, Maurice, who encouraged me in this project and Father M, who looked over some of the pieces and who gave me some useful prompts for 'Ave' which helped me to improve it.

Michael Lewis Owen

Introduction

Pass through the Open Door and Choose (Ann Hughes)

Come Barefoot

A: The Story Begins

1. Trinity Father 📻 *'O Lux Beata Trinitas', The original Gregorian Chant*
2. Adam: 'Why Did I?'
3. Moses, Barefoot, at the Burning Bush
4. David a Boy Faces the Mighty Goliath
5. Elijah
6. Hannah
7. Ruth
8. Trinity Son 📻 *'O Lux Beata Trinitas', William Byrd: Gregorian Chant*
9. Susanna and Daniel
10. Darius and Daniel
11. Trinity Spirit 📻 *'O Lux Beata Trinitas', Andrej   Makor: Gregorian Chant*

   📻 *Christoph Gluck: Dance of The Blessed Spirits for flute and piano (Orpheus & Eurydice)*

B: Good News

Advent, Christmas and the Boyhood of Jesus

12. Gabriel's Message for Zechariah
13. Ave ♫ *Franz Schubert: Ave Maria, Maria Callas*
14. Pregnant Cousins ♫ *Orlando Gibbons: Magnificat,*
    Choir of King's College Cambridge
    Mary Visits Elizabeth
15. Gabriel Prompts Joseph
16. Birth of John the Baptist
17. Hurrying Shepherds ♫ *G. F. Handel: Messiah,*
    For Unto Us a Child is Born 174
18. Which Path to Choose?
    Wise Men's Way, or Joseph's or Herod's?
19. Enlightenment
    Simeon Recognises the Messiah
20. At the Temple
    A rare glance at Jesus the Boy
21. Joy of John the Baptist

Miracles

Sinners

Holy Week Easter Ascension Pentecost

Mindfulness

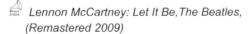
Prayers

Closure but leave the door ajar

George Harrison: Here Comes the Sun, The Beatles (2019 Mix)

Appendix

Biblical references for each piece

Introduction

Pass through the Open Door and Choose

Come on a journey now – are you game?

Follow from the start or choose your own path!

Your heart can lead; it's sure to find the way.

You may encounter light, shade, emotions

That may thrill or chill your every bone.

You'll meet persons of note as you go,

Ordinary people too like me and you.

Let's take you on a journey which may open-up your mind,

A crack at least and maybe more,

Sharing wonders, marvels, hopes, truths,

A rich seam of insights to explore.

These touch upon pure peace and strife,

Wide aspects of all human life.

So, when do we begin this trip? And what will we need?

The doors open wide - come, cross the threshold ….

Come Barefoot

Deep down you know, don't you?

Feel deep within and remember:
The ripples of happiness sweet
That come with actions of kindness;
The sudden joy that smiles brightly
Unseen perhaps but welling deep.

Feel deep within and touch upon:
That rich peace which abides there
A peace beyond all reasoning
A peace that exudes and includes
Enveloping everything.

Deep down you know, don't you?

Children of the light
Come barefoot
Carry your shoes
And come inside.

A   The Story Begins

1   Trinity Trilogy Father

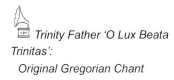 *Trinity Father 'O Lux Beata Trinitas':*
Original Gregorian Chant

Father creator
Riding eternity at ease
Ever bringing life

2   Adam: 'Why Did I?'

Why did I bite it?
Knew that I should not,
Knew that it meant death
And was forbidden.

It was the woman
She gave me the fruit.
This my explanation
Exonerates not.

Was it sweetest Eve,
Really, was it her?
How quick I was, caught,
To flip it onto her.

I knew the command,
Heard the serpent's words,
Saw Eve was unharmed
And made up my mind.

What enticed us there,
To learn right and wrong
And to be like gods
With eyes wide open?

I heard you and hid,
Afraid, found at fault,
My fault
Disobedience.

3   Moses Barefoot at the Burning Bush

The bush is blazing
Aflame

Mystified
He approaches

It is whole
Untouched

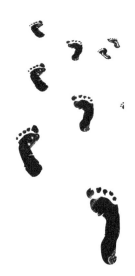

He stops
Removes his shoes

Covers his eyes
And hides his face
Because he
Dare not look

4   David a Boy Faces the Mighty Goliath

On his head is a bronze helmet,
Massive he stands before all.
Scale armour covers his broad breast
And on his shoulder rests his spear.

We know of his boastful challenge,
His offer of single combat
Before both of the great armies
And of his scorn for all of us.

From our ranks rising like the sun,
Light as air and like a fresh breeze,
The lad so pleasant to look upon
Springs forth, armourless is he.

With angry frown the giant rants
As he looks down upon the boy:
A mere plaything, a boy to bash,
A stick to snap over his knee.

He comes with sword and spear - colossal -
To make an easy kill for bird food,
This puny boy is done for now -
Then the smooth stone stuns him silent.

5   Elijah

The jar of meal won't go empty
And the jug of oil will not fail

Elijah's voice rings round truly
And the widow's son comes alive

The ox of Baal lies ignored
While Elijah's the fire consumes

Into the wilderness he goes
Sick at heart afraid and spent

Told to get up and eat
He does

Gains strength for the lonely journey

Into the cave alone he goes
The only one left - so he thinks

The strong wind shakes the high mountain
And earthquake shatters its rocks
A fire is burning
Crackling loud
A gentle breeze comes

And he hides

Go back
He must go back

Return
And anoint the next in line

At last the chariot of fire
Takes him

And his cloak falls ...

Falls there

6   Hannah

In bitterness and tears of salt,
I ask you to bear me in mind
And to take notice of my words,
I, who am lowly and distressed.

No razor shall touch one small hair
Given for all life up to you.

I am not a worthless woman
Just a maidservant who is true.

Speaking from the depth of my grief,
Expressing my resentment here
Openly and for your favour,
Hoping to find it in your sight.

*   *   *

Here is the one; the one asked for.
Here is he:
My son,
My only one.

Given to you, given back now,
Made over for all his life here.

My heart exults, I rejoice.
Lowly, as I am, he lifts me
To a place beside the richest,
He gives me a seat of honour.

Great things he has done for me now;
My hunger he has filled today.

He safeguards my steps in the dark
As his maidservant dances.

7   Ruth

A young woman of truth
Bends low to the barley
On her feet from morning
Gleaning behind reapers
Among the sheaves themselves

A young woman of truth
Bending low to the ground
Earning notice and more
A foreigner she is
Better than seven sons

A young woman of truth
Eating some of his bread
Dipping into his wine
Fine she is but humble
Ready to serve without check

A young woman of truth
Bringing food to give her
Food for her mother-in-law
A better daughter true
Than many who are loved

A young woman of truth
Taking all the advice
Under his feet all the night
Beneath the hem of his cloak
Waiting upon her lord

A young woman of truth
Honourably taken
A wife again far from home
A mother now as well
Up from the threshing-floor

A son
A comfort true
A prop for one's old age
A child to perpetuate
To carry the line down

Grandfather to David

8   Trinity Trilogy Son

 *Trinity Son, William Byrd: 'O Lux Beata Trinitas'*

Son the beloved one
Our most noble saviour
And our dear brother

9   Susanna and Daniel

Sweet Susanna fair
Walks the garden gracefully
 Beauty unaware

Male elders plotting
Chasing after wrong desires
So unwholesomely

Force her to lie there
Taste such a sweet innocent
Or lie about her

Innocence cries out
Deceit and slander holler
 Beauty is accused

Elders are believed
Beauty is taken to stone
Daniel cries out

Questions follow close
By which tree was she lying
During her sinning

Elder A is first
'Twas under the mastic tree
He lies brazenly

Elder B is next
They sinned beneath the holm oak
He lies openly

Elders are exposed
Everyone sees the same truth
Beauty freely goes

10   Darius and Daniel

They could find nothing against him,
Nothing to discredit him at all.
Never was he negligent;
All his service was clear,
Without a fault - outstandingly
Good.

Trap him they would, if they knew how,
Or he would be over them all
And rule the kingdom, the whole of it,
On behalf of the king himself.

So they devised their careful plot
For him.

Appeal to the king's great weakness,
Smooth him sleek with oily flattery
And have him declare an edict strict:
That all must pray to Darius alone
For thirty days, on pain of prison
In the lions' cave.

The edict is written out clear
And King Darius signs at once,
But still Daniel in his room
Prays thrice daily to his God.

There he is taken and brought down
To Darius, the regal king.

Too late he sees the danger now,
With the edict broken he must act.

Distressed indeed, Darius racks his brains
For an escape.
Your God sees your faith;
He will save you.

His look is pure and seems to say:
I have never done you a wrong
O king.

Into the lions' den they thrust him
A massive, mighty boulder rolls
Over the black mouth it goes.

The sorrowful king then returns
To watch alone and fast and hope.

No harm to Daniel ensues:
The great lions, with angelic sense,
Seem to smell his clear innocence.

When Darius in the morning
Runs to ask, *Has your God saved you?*
He finds Daniel has not been hurt,
Has not been hurt in any way.

The boulder
Massive
Is pulled back

Heave and heave
And down away now

Then Daniel rises
From the cave.

11   Trinity Trilogy Spirit

 Trinity Spirit, Andrej Makor: 'O Lux Beata Trinitas'

Spirit of strong light
Homing sure within our hearts
With soft wings of hope

 Christoph Gluck: Dance of The Blessed Spirits for flute & piano.

B   Good News

Advent   Christmas

The Boyhood of Jesus

12   Gabriel's Message for Zechariah

The angel of the lord makes me start up.
Dreams are unfolding here now before me.
My wife to bear a son, he will be great
And bring such joy to me and all besides.

He will turn them back, return them to good:
Call the hearts of fathers to their children,
Bring the nation back to truth and virtue -
Back to wisdom - to a fit way of life.

Doubt claws at my mind, is it possible?
Elizabeth's getting on and I'm old.
Can I be sure? Can I be certain?
What surety of this can you give me?

I hear that he is Gabriel sent here
To speak to me and bring this good news.
I must listen and trust and lose my speech
Until this, all happens, just as he says.

Out I go to the people waiting there,
I cannot speak for joy, I cannot speak.
I can only make signs to them
And remain without words, silent.

13   **Ave**

There she is!
Youthful and sweet
And so humble.

Dare I approach?
Just listen.
Such soft singing,
Lipping, lapping
From her very soul.

The well water
Springs from depth
Cool, clear and good.
Oh yes that strain
Again and again -
Her breathless song.

In awe I am
But have to go
To speak, to break
The message entrusted.

Just look upon her
There:
Pure
Perfect
Peacefulness personified.
Must I disturb
that?

Mark how she works:
Caringly
Carefully
Ceaselessly
Caressingly and calm.

This is my hardest,
Most honourable
But most trying
Task.

Perceive her thoughts:
Fair
Fairer than fair
Fairest

Full of grace
Forever good
Immaculate.

Hail! Hail Mary! …

The Hail Mary

Hail Mary, full of grace,
the Lord is with thee:
Blessed art thou among women...

Yr Henffych Well

Henffych well, Fair, gyflawn o ras,
y mae'r Arglwydd gyda thi;
Bendigedig wyt ymhlith merched...

Ave Maria: Franz Schubert, Maria Callas

14 Pregnant Cousins

(Mary visits Elizabeth)

She goes as quickly as she can.
It is hill country and rocky,
Hard to travel, a dust filled track
That turns its long length all the way.

The joy of greeting fills her heart,
A leap of spirits for both,
With their rich burdens so heavy
And so sweet, so new to this earth.

Most blessed indeed is the bliss here,
Heaven on earth in the sunshine.
Their eyes gleam in recognition;
Such joy after the long dry road.

A soft breeze caresses them there,
A ripple, within, stirs their souls
As they feel the great deed of love
And the baby leaps, quick with joy.

Magnificat: Orlando Gibbons, Choir of King's College, Cambridge

15 The Carpenter's Dilemma

His mind is set
But wrongly so;
I must change it
Help him see.

Soft, he sleeps there!
I must approach.
I see his soul,
Divine it is.
So richly marked,
Fills me with awe.
A very good man
Though needing my aid.

Joseph! Joseph!
She is with child
Sinless and pure;
You must take her;
Keep her truly.

Joseph! Joseph!
Her child is great,
The Saviour,
The one promised:
Emmanuel.

16   Birth of John the Baptist

All is possible and we have a son!

Good people suggest his name should
Be Zechariah, after me.
My Elizabeth says, *He is called John.*
I write upon my slate; *His name is John.*

At that instant, my speech returns to me,
To the astonishment of all present.

Our son will go before to prepare us
For the rising sun and light of life,
The gentle shepherd of peaceful ways.

17   Hurrying Shepherds

So, they hurry, of course they do,
After the glory in the night
Out in the country far and wide,
High in the hills and mountains.

Terrifyingly brilliant lightning
Rending the dark sky into pieces;
Singing to pierce the hardest heart.
Pure and urgent: 'Listen. Listen!'

Glistening, their eyes watch it all
As they stiffen and hearken, keen
To hear everything, each cadence,
And to grasp the whole of the strain.

Not just any child, not at all -
Simply there in the manger, still,
As they rush to a stop and stand:

Alleluja! Alleluja!

*Handel's Messiah, For unto Us a Child is Born:
Megaron Baroque Orchestra & Choir, Ljubljana*

18   Which Path to Choose?

(Wise Men's way, or Joseph's or Herod's?)

His star is rising.

Cross country they ride
By night and by day
Eyes ever on it.

As they journey hard
Joseph is deciding,
Quietly, informally,
To just let her go.

Close by, powerful,
And too frightened
To choose the right way
A king plots murder.

His star is twinkling.
While Joseph ponders,
A man of honour
Seeking the best way.
His star is blazing.
As Joseph dreams deep
Into the bright night
Not to be afraid.

Onwards they travel
With rich gifts of gold
Of frankincense
And fragrant myrrh.

Under the starlight
Homage rare they pay
And journey home
By another way.

Another way too
For Joseph right now,
Dreaming their escape
While far shines the star.

His star is highest.
There!
Still.

Raining diamonds
On the Son below.

19   Enlightenment
(Simeon Recognises the Messiah)

See! They bring turtle doves
And the boy child, see how they come:
Unsure yet together,
Tired but brimming in light within.

Now Simeon is standing
Upright, he is, and true.
He takes the child into his arms.
His long wait, he knows, has ended
When he holds Jesus close,
Right there in his heart.

She looks on in wonder,
Thinking, What *is happening here?*

The child keeps still arms wide,
As the devout man looks to her.

My eyes have seen, he says,
And then, A *light to enlighten.*

What might it mean? she breathes
And takes these words right to heart.

Then he speaks of a sign rejected
And a sword that will pierce -
His words as shadows cross
They weigh heavy upon her
And she feels her heart reeling.

Now Anna is there praising all,
Aged she is but still strong,
And looks upon the child in awe,
Her eyes and soul, praising.

See - they go from the holy place.
Still together, still unsure,
Still brimming with that inner light
While Mary is sifting all.

20   At the Temple
(A rare glance of Jesus the Boy)

Surely, surely, surely he is with them
In the caravan, the social party,
All relaxing after the happy feast.
He's at that friendly age, well grown and strong.

Let him find his feet and grow a little.
Surely, surely, surely he will be back.
Back to us, back with us in the morning,
Now he is among friends talking freely.

Not to be found, not in the caravan,
Never with them, gone for a whole day and night!
So unlike him, not like him - not at all.
We cannot keep calm; cannot carry on.

Back, we must hurry all the way all day.
Surely, surely, surely he is not far -
But where has he gone and why would he go?
We must go quickly and find him today.

Through the city we go searching for him:
Neither sight nor sign of him can we find
And the rising disquiet is pounding fast.
Surely, surely, surely he must be here.

On the third day, in daylight,
We see him sitting, listening and talking,
A boy discoursing among doctors,
Learned beyond his years, careless of our cares.

Quite overcome,
Open mouthed,
We stand and watch.

Mary moving to him says, *My child, why?*

He looks her in the eye, Don't *you know?*
Surely, surely, surely you know, don't you?

21   The Baptist's Joy

How can I explain it to them?

I am a man born of the earth
Sent before him, posted in front,
To prepare the way for the one
Now here.   I'm not the way myself
But understand, know, that he is.

He is here so I grow smaller;
My time is over and complete.

This is my joy: to know he's come,
To hear of his work and his words,
To accept his testimony
That comes, direct from heaven.

I feel joy so great to hear him.
My heart is full. It surges high
When he, on his way, is passing.

How can I explain it to you?
My joy in his presence abounds
Just as I leapt in the womb.

Miracles

22   Six Stone Jars
(Water into Wine)

All were there of course:
Joseph in the corner amongst them
Laughing and smiling
Andrew and Philip are in their cups -
And watching everything is Mary.

She recalls it well:
The six stone jars
The servants and guests
And Jesus, her son,
Away from himself, at ease.

Clearly reviews it:
The jars, the wine, the water -
The dangers there also,
But all will be fine here now,
Better than ever, see.

She calls Jesus to himself,
His hour has not come
But she calls him nonetheless
And he shrugs as if to say:
Why bother me now?

Enough -
She turns to the servants:
Do everything he asks of you.

23   How Many Miracles Do We Need?

If someone can
Make water flow
Shall they drink it?

If someone does
Make the sun dance
Will they notice?

If someone may
Feed the hungry
How about that?

The rich man begs
To warn his kin
Might they see then?

If someone should
Rise from the dead
Would they listen?

24   My Leprosy Is Cured!

I know it is in his gift now
And I watch him closely for sure.
There he descends, a crowd behind,
Down from the mountain he comes.

I kneel and bow, lower my head
And hold out my leprous fingers,
If you want to you can cure,
I say in low supplication.

Of course I want to, he replies,
And touches me, touches me just so,
Touches all the way, right through me,
Passing straight to my open soul.

Cured!

Pressing a finger to his lips
He points for me to go, now whole.
Free at last, I walk easily
And freely, freely pour my heart.

25   Peter Walks on Water

Now in the fourth watch of the night
We see a figure on the dark shore,
Black in the night sky, standing there.
The swell is heavy with the wind;
The waves surge, lifting and dying.

Stark - so odd, so weird to see
The figure's approach, slow but sure.
We fear it, so strange and dark -

Is it a ghost?

The lake churns and the cold wind moans.

It is me. Do not be afraid.

With a leap of my heart I know
It is the Lord who is coming.
Out of the boat I go at once,
Out of my depth upon the lake.

I walk as if upon firm ground
Until the wind rouses my doubt
And then I am sinking straight down,
Lost, and completely foundering.

So, he holds me and lifts me clear.

 Løvland & Graham: You Raise Me Up, Josh Groban

26   Jesus Transformed before Our Eyes

Yes, the three of us saw it all.

High up the mountain, after him,
We climbed the dry-stone way, alone.

High up to the blue
Just hard rock
And sky

That was the setting.

There upon the mountain, alone
With Moses, Elijah and us.

The light
The fire
The radiance

Yes, it is true, completely true,
His face shone with fire, burning bright.

Sheer brilliance - and Peter starts
Babbling about making three tents
And we three fill with fear right there.

Then, a bright cloud throws us a cloak:
This is my Son, the Beloved …
Listen to him.

27   Jesus Weeps then Raises Lazarus

He does many good works for all to see;
For which of them do they prepare their
stones?

They say it is for *wicked blasphemy.*

We shimmer in the haze and go from there.

Now he stops and turns his steps back to them
Asking if there are not twelve hours of the day,
Time enough to walk their way again,
Time enough to help his dear, resting friend.

He is pleased we were not there to see it
Since now we can be brought into belief.

*   *   *

Beloved Lazarus is newly dead
So Martha meets us on that sun hot road.
She tells Jesus she knows he is the Christ
Then calls for her sister, Mary, to come
That the Master is here and he wants her.

No ointment now …
                          Mary's tears wash his feet.
Her sadness and everyone's sorrow

Afflict him, distress him sorely -
Sighing
The words, he sadly breathes:
Where have you put him?

All are moved, deeply so, and Jesus weeps.

See how he loves them Martha and Mary
And their brother too, his departed friend,
Four days dead, dearly beloved, Lazarus.
The rock is rolled away -
Dark now open mouthed.

We stand in wonder and watch with eyes wide.

Our ears hear the cry.

His call pierces all
As out, up from the darkness –
Lazarus comes!

 Howard Goodall: Psalm 23, The Lord is my Shepherd,
St Paul's Cathedral Choir,

28   My Withered Hand Straightened on the Sabbath

I am there
He teaches near
He sees me
Feelingly

They are watching him too
But not in a good manner
They hope to outwit him
Down him and catch him out.

He is here
Looking clear
Towards me
Gently see

He knows their very thoughts
He knows their ways and wiles
He knows the law and more
He knows it's the sabbath

He calls me
Caringly
Tenderly
Lovingly

They see my withered hand
As I stand before him
They watch it straightening
On the sabbath - just so

He looks on
The whole scene
Their anger
My deep bliss

I am there
Still so near
Deep within
I feel him.

29   Born Blind

We know he is our son
We know he was born blind;
We don't know how it is
Or who opened his eyes.

Let him speak for himself;
He might tell you it all.
Ask him how it happens
That born blind he now sees.

He does not tell of the
Musical lilt, the tone,
The spirit soothing sound,
The sweet words within.

He cannot tell them that part.

They are blind, unseeing,
Hard of heart - threatening -
As he looks upon them.
They cannot hear the truth
Or bear to see it there
Revealed before them all

Cured, he understands.

John Newton: Amazing Grace, Judy Collins with Boys' Choir of Harlem

30 At the Seventh Hour

I feel fearful all right.
My son has reached death's door
And I am fearing the worst,
Away from home on duty.

Come down, Sir, I implored,
Before my child dies. Come.

There Jesus looked at me
And commanded me home.

Belief in him filled me.
He said my son would live
And more at ease I went
To begin my journey.

Now! Approaching fast, I see -
Members of my household
Hurrying to meet me.

Do I fear or believe?

I stand and tremble.
What is the news from home?

Their high held heads bring hope
As does their striding gait.

Yesterday, the man says,
The fever left him safe.
It was the seventh hour.

Now I am trembling more.

For at the seventh hour,
Yesterday he said it:
Your son will live.
Go home.

31   Danger on the Water
(Jesus Calms the Storm)

Without warning
It is on us.
Wild wind whistles
Raising our fear!

The waters grow,
Surface whitens
As the waves lap,
Slap on the hull.

Into the boat
Waters now crash;
High above us
They rush downwards.

Again, they surge,
Violent and strong.
We cower down
While he sleeps on.

We're going down!
Save us! Save us!

He wakes then stands
To look around.
Outstretched fingers
He raises up
Into the sky.

Why be afraid?

He rebukes them:
The wind and sea.
Down
     Down they drop.
          Calmed.
              Stilled.
                  Jesusfied.

 *Løvland/Graham: You Raise Me Up, Aled Jones*

32   Healed beside the Pool
(Tut-tut, would you believe it, Jesus working on the holy day?)

Alone with no helper
I struggle towards it
The healing pool but too slow

Do you want to be well?

His question rouses me
And his look searches deep

He tells me simply this:
Pick up your sleeping mat.

I do so and am whole

Today is the sabbath
And I carry my mat
As instructed by him

They say it is not right
I should not carry it
On this most holy day

He warns me
Of my life

He tells me
To be true

Or much worse will happen

He tells them
He copies
The way of his Father
Who is working today

33   How Often Do We Thank?
(All Ten Lepers are Cured)

How must it feel?
I wonder ….

All ten are cured at the same time
Cured
Cleansed from loathsome leprosy
And only one gives thanks
Only one mind

How must it feel?
I wonder….

Where are the other nine? he inquires
Knowing full well what we are like
Quick to ask but so slow to thank

How deeply it must reach within -
More thankless than a serpent's tooth -
And after all the gifts of grace
Freely cleansing our guiltiness

How must it feel
I wonder?

34   Certainly Completely Blind

(Saul Becomes Paul)

I am taken by the hand,
Blind certainly, completely blind.

I so sure of myself
Not so now -
Not so now
As I stumble low.

I so wise
Just so ignorant.

They take my arm along the way.
All is dark to my broken sight.

All is right now
When all was wrong:
The wrong highway -
A blind alley.

Now unseeing
I go
Seeing at last.

Ah!

The light all over the place
Within
Without
Above
Below
Utterly amazing
And wild.

Truly a baptism of fire
So bright
So fiercely blinding my sight.

Oh!

His voice so urgent and sharp
Authoritative
And so clear
Loud
And imperiously crisp
Leaving no doubt
Not a shadow
Not a scruple.

Why stone them?
Why do I seek their destruction?

I am down
Ground down
Very low
Listening
And
Seeing!

Free at last
My spirit perceives
Knows
And already understands.

So
Now they take me by the hand
Completely changed
Transformed
Saved
And on my way
To Damascus.

35 Uneasy
(The Apostles Cure the Aged Cripple)

It is simply a kindness.
They talk to an old, male cripple
And he stands up, perfectly sound.

What of that?
Why does it disturb?

The stone rejected by us all;
They now proclaim as keystone.

Such audacity - brazen too -
To flout our revered authority!

Amazing is their outspokenness
With the cured one standing beside.
They undo the order of all.

How do we act
To stop its spread?

Inside, inaudible are the doubts,
Deep and dark, that lurk unbidden.

What are we going to do now
With these uneducated men?

36 Senseless as Your Leaders

(Peter Cures the Beggar)

You had no idea what you did
When you demanded his own life

Just as senseless as your leaders
You called for the murderer's reprieve

Now you run here all excited
You race to the Beautiful Gate

Standing whole
Standing up alone
You see the man
You know so well

Here he sits all day
Asking alms
He sees us
And holds out his cup

We have neither
Silver nor gold
Peter takes his hands
And now he stands

Look at us
Wretches everyone

Walk whole with Christ
The risen one

37   Plenty

Bread to your hearts' content
Abundant as the rain
That falls in time of flood

Bread to your hearts' content

Water for your thirst too
Struck from the rock running
Pure and clear, cool and fresh

Water for your thirst too

Bread, yes loaves for all here
All will have plenty now
More than enough children

Bread, yes loaves for all here

Wine for all the people

For those who have no wine
Plenty now of the best

Wine for all the people
The bread of life for all

Come, come, come -
All who hunger
All who thirst
Come now

The bread of life for all

G.F.Handel's Messiah: He Shall Feed His Flock,
Renee Fleming

Sinners

38 **A Woman of Many Husbands**
(At the Well)

I tell him he has no bucket
And the well's deep beyond my reach.

He asks without even a word -
Just looks upon me openly:
He wants to share my refreshment.

Living water is what he has
But no bucket to draw it up
And the well sinks round, down below.

Deeply he looks upon me
And asks me to call my husband.

I have none, I say colouring.

And he gazes deeper within
And seems to uncover all five.

Gently he inclines his forehead:
I know that is the truth, he says.

He tells me about his water
Which turns to a spring, welling here,
Deep within my very being.

Whilst he speaks, everything I am
Spills out for him and me to see.

As he says the words, I *am he,*
I know he is the only way.

I hurry back to town at that,
To tell my friends my new found truth,
Leaving more than my drinking jar.

39 Caught in Adultery

He is sitting there teaching them
And I am brought forward, ashamed.
Of course I am low and downcast
Caught in the act as you say.

I am frightened too, really scared
As I know the hard penalty
That is sure to come my way now.

They make me stand there in full view -

And slowly he looks them over,
Seeming to reach deep into them
With his long look at each in turn.

Master, they call him, all upright,
Indignant in tone about me,
My wickedness, my perfidy.

With his finger in the dry sand
He begins writing, carefully.

Can they see?
Can they understand?

Quietly,
Ever so quietly,
He speaks his momentous response,
Gently speaking, while I tremble.

If there is one of you, alone,
Just one, who has no sinfulness,
Let him come and throw the first stone.

Then he resumes his careful work.

I cringe and await the first blow
But beginning with the eldest
They turn, withdraw and go.

Now, he lifts his eyes up to mine
As I stand before him there, just me.

Has no-one condemned you? he asks,

And I feel it flowing into me there
His pure compassion easing my sin.

I stand before him there, alone,
Before the light of the world
And I see that I can follow him
Accepting the light of life.

Then he writes some more in the sand
And I am free,
Completely free
To go on my way and to live.

40 Zacchaeus Is Swept to Safety

What does he desire?
What can he be like?

I'm too fat and short,
So I'm running on
To find a stout tree
Growing by the way.

Up, up to the top - now
I will see him soon.
As he passes by,
I will catch a glimpse.

I can hear the crowd.
He must be close.

Look!
Coming into view, there!
Closer!
He is here now!

Oh!

He stops beneath
And looks up at me;
And I'm swept away
From myself for sure.

He will dine with me
Today
At my table.

I must climb right down
And hurry off home.

Great change is in me:

I'm giving my wealth away,
Repaying the cheated,
My salvation's come.

41   The Greater the Forgiveness the Deeper the Love

Her reputation's bad.
We know all about her
Yet here she approaches.

Close to him
At his feet

Weeping upon his toes,
Her heartfelt tears falling
Fast upon him, she sobs.

And he allows her there

Now she is wiping them,
Using her hair like a cloth,
Polishing his damp feet.

And he lets her do it

Covering his feet, look,
All over with kisses,
Kissing again, again -

Still he gives her leave

Out comes the ointment, see,
Costly and so precious
But she anoints his feet.

And he does not stay her

Her reputation's bad
But her devotion's great;
She knows his forgiveness
In its richest giving.

The Master eyes her -   look!
His gaze, it's so loving.

42   The Spendthrift Son
(A Servant's Monologue)

'Coming from the fields he calls me
And asks what it is all about.

Where to begin? I ask myself -
A mere servant to inform the eldest son!

He can hear it:
       The music clear
       That rolls on the air,
       Joyously -
And he can see:
       The movements light
       Of the dancing
       Of their quick limbs.

I hear the young master
And see his bewilderment.

"While still far off the lad was seen
Far away below, a mere spot,
Walking the dusty, winding road.

Just before he came into sight,
The watcher sensed his approach
And started up, straining to see.

At once he leaps, like a young man,
And down from his high place races
In a river of joy,

Trembling.
Emotion filled from head to heart
To greet his son the father runs.

The boy stands with eyes that glisten.
He hardly dares to hope or look.
Down at heel in every way:
Dirt stained, unwashed, undeserving,
He stands with limp hands unfurled.

My father, I have faults to tell …
But no more than that is spoken
The strong embrace absolves the wrongs.
There! On the open road in clear sight
They make their peace for all to see."

Still the young master looks perplexed
So I bluntly say:

"Your missing brother has come back
And your father is rejoicing
Since his lost son has just been found,
And has returned home both safe and sound."

 *Yusuf/Cat Stevens:*
Father and Son

Holy Week   Easter

Ascension   Pentecost

43   **Look!**
(Palms at the Ready He's Passing By)

Look!
The whole world
Is running
After him
Look!

Look!
There riding
On the colt
Astride it
Look!

Look!
A huge crowd
Follows him
As he goes
Look!

Look!
Palms strewn there
On the road
Hosanna
Look!

Look!
He's passing
On his way
Here just now
Look!

44 The Hour Has Come
(Jesus Prepares to Suffer and Die)

I know the hour has come.

The grain must fall to the ground
Or bear no fruit at all;
Grounded, it bears plenty.

My soul is much oppressed.

What shall I say or do?
Ask for deliverance
Or give, give everything?

When lifted from the earth
All shall come, drawn to me.

45 He Washes Each Foot
(Maundy Thursday)

The hour is here
Close and heavy
Upon him.

He looks around.

His eyes
Hurting with love
Take everyone in.

He comes to each in turn.

Takes each foot in his hands
And the wave of love
Folds to the floor.

The water surprises
It is warm
And soothing - cool.

The cloth
Is gentle.
His touch
A caress.

Still
Locked in time
A moment
That draws into
Eternity
Our eyes meet.

Mine look down
To his
Depth
Of
Compassion.

Peter
Is
Embarrassed:

No, no, no
Master
Never!

Gently
Kindly
He is persuaded;
And feels
The water's
Pure
Kiss.

46   Outside
(The Last Supper)

We look each at the other ones.
Jesus seems troubled.

What does it mean?

We are here dining together
Sharing our bread
Sharing our wine.

The night is coming down quickly ….

But slowly, outside of it all,
He wields the bread and dips it in

As the darkness is coming down fast.

One of us leaves;
Goes from the room.
The night is fallen;
Dark it is.

Inside, we draw breath and listen
Like the little children we are.

Our hearts sense and feel his trouble.
He knows the way we cannot go.

He knows the way and is the way,
The only way we can follow.

How can we follow in the dark?

He is going soon,
Very soon.

We feel it
Pressing upon us.
The hour we fear;
It's nearly here.

47   I Am He
(The Sacrificial Lamb)

I am he.

They draw back
And fall down.

I am he
In purple
All prepared.

Just take me.
Leave them all;
I've lost none.

I am he
To condemn
Scourge and crown.

They are mine.

Lambs and sheep
Come to me.

I will be
The scapegoat
Saviour.

It is from
My Father
That I come.

I'm the one,
The beloved
Faithful son.

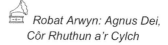 *Robat Arwyn: Agnus Dei,*
Côr Rhuthun a'r Cylch

48 Kingship

(Good Friday Saviour)

So much mockery

The crown of thorns
Scorns
And the purple robe
Titters and sniggers
At kingship lampooned

Save yourself

They jeer
The leaders and crowd

Save yourself

They sneer
The soldiers on guard

Save yourself O King!
Cries the hanging thief

Beneath the scoffing
Below all the scorn
Sadly standing close
Mourn a group forlorn

Even now like this
He saves one more
Look
One hanging beside
Who sees and utters

This man did no wrong

And suddenly prays

When in your kingdom
Remember me Jesus

49   My God My God
(Psalm 22)

My God, my God, why have you deserted me?

My tongue sticks to my jaw
My palate a dry dish;
My heart melting like wax.
I am water drying,
Water draining away
Into the dust of death.

My God! My God!
All day I call,
I cry all night
Your ear to catch.

All who see jeer at me;
They toss their heads to sneer;
They cast lots for my clothes.

Save me from the lion's mouth;
From the paws of the dog
And the horns of the bulls
Rescue my poor soul.

You hide not your face.
You fail not the poor man
When he calls but answer him.

The whole earth comes to you;
All peoples bow to you;
The powerful bend low;
All who are dust come too.

My soul shall live for you;
My children serve you;
Generations to come,
People yet to be born
Will acclaim you, my God.

All this you have done.

50   At the Foot
(Good Friday Mourners)

There at the foot they stand:
The wife of Clopas weeps
And Mary of Magdala.

Next to them, so very still,
Ashen faced, her eyes raised,
Stands His mother, Mary.

Liquid sky, inky, glum,
The air is tart and moist.

John is to her side,
The beloved disciple.

Jesus speaks lowly,
This is your mother.

The thunder clouds threaten
And He awaits, thirsty.

They have no water now.
They have nothing:
No wine -
Sour and sharp, acrid air
And vinegar from a jar.

Bowing his head he says:
It is accomplished.

He gives up his spirit.

There on the hill
They stand,
Beloved,
Bereft,
Alone
As the light darkens.

51   Giving without Costing

(The Generosity of Jesus)

In the Kedron Valley
There was a garden there
Which the traitor knew well
Where Jesus went to pray

Bringing their lanterns
Carrying their torches
Bearing their weapons
They came down upon him

The guards seized him fiercely
Bound him and took him off
With them he went in peace
In his whole innocence

Giving without costing

They led him next morning
And questioned all he is
Demanded answers from him
And there he stood by truth

Giving them his patience

They shouted and they hissed
They had him taken out
To scourge and mock and slap
And there he endured it

Giving them his sorrow

He carried his own cross
Tasted their vinegar
And bowed his head to die
Giving his spirit there

Giving his forgiveness

 Refrain – Robat Arwyn: Agnus Dei,
Côr Rhuthun a'r Cylch

52   There
(Good Friday Reflections)

Before bare-faced Pilate
He stands

Bearing his cross bravely
He goes

Up the bare mountainside
He works

Stripped bare of his clothes
He gasps

Nailed by bare hands and feet
He loves

Bearing everything there
He dies

53   Myrrh and Aloes

(Good Friday Burial)

It is a peaceful place nearby
In a garden just below.

Now here comes Joseph, true of heart,
Of Arimathaea as they say
His sandaled feet hasten to Pilate.

Afraid and sensibly fearful,
He knows to conceal his belief.

We have a new tomb near that spot
Hewn from the rock and ready
With your permission …

Joseph holds his trembling breath,
Still he stands.

His head is bowed
And long it seems to him
The wait,
The permission that he craves.

Pilate nods.

A clean linen cloth all laid out
And spices - myrrh and aloes -
And a second cloth for his head,
All are ready, all waiting there.

It is a peaceful place nearby
In a garden just below.

Beside the opening
Stands
A massive boulder
Cold and rough
And ready to roll.

 *Refrain – Robat Arwyn: Agnus
Dei, Côr Rhuthun a'r Cylch*

54   May I?
(Mary of Magdala Accompanies Jesus)

May I stand with you?

I feel you shudder
As the words:
Take him away! Take him away!
Hurt your heart and mine.

May I stand with you,
Mary of Magdala?

Of course we don't -
What an absurd question!

Wash your hands all you can;
Wash and weep.
You are handing him on,
Red-handed Pilate.

Oh!
But even Peter
Betrays him.
Three times Peter
Denies him.
Warms himself before the fire
And says:
I am not.

May I stand near you
Beneath that sign -

The pity of it

May I, Mary of Magdala?

Look at his clothes
In piles of four
As booty.

A touch of his hem would
Cure -
Oh look at it now
And weep.

May I stand with you?
He is thirsty.
Come to the water all you who
Thirst, though you have - nothing!
Nothing.

His head is bowing,
May I stand beside you,
Mary of Magdala?

It is dark
But may I run with you,
Mary of Magdala?

The long, sorrowful night is passing
May I run with you?

Can I turn round with you,
Mary of Magdala?

Can I speak to him too?

Would I recognise him,
Mary of Magdala?

Will he greet me by name,
Mary?

55 Unsure

(John Begins to See in the Empty Tomb)

That blurry feeling
Dryness in the mouth
Weary sleeplessness
After wretchedness

Living the nightmare
The mind reels darkly
And dry swallows fly
Down in air pockets

Running she comes to us
Her words rush from her
And send us tearing
Away on the hill

Panting and waiting
I stand there - outside
Until Peter comes
And runs straight inside

I peer in the dark
Unsure uncertain
As I see the cloths
Lying on the ground

The one from his head
Has been rolled right up
And placed by itself -
Neatly put aside

My mouth is so dry
I cannot swallow
As I begin there
To see in the dark

56   Out of the Dark

(Jesus Has Risen)

Pitter patter, hear,
Light feet coming near.

Light foot Mary, see -
Through the gloom running,
Hastening to us.

Now out of the dark
She bursts lightly in
And stops, stands and breathes
Fast and shallow gasps
Here with us, alone.

They have taken him.
The Lord is not there.
We do not know where
They have gone with him;
He's not in the tomb.

Wide-eyed, Peter stands.

Then we run at speed
Together at first
But soon Peter is
Far behind my lead.

Catching breath I stoop
And look into it.

The tomb is dark, void -
Save for a few cloths,
Neat, piled in place.

Peter's breath is warm.
He pats the boulder,
Massive, out of place,
Beside the entrance.
Then in he hurries.

I follow at once.

The Lord is not there.

I feel the hairs burst
Across my body
And know the real truth.

Alleluja begins
To ring, hallelujah
Starts to sing within,
Alleluja today.

 *Leonard Cohen: Hallelujah!*
Rufus Wainwright

57 The Garden Tomb

(Mary of Magdala Runs into the Risen Lord)

Weeping on the hillside,
She awaits the dawning.

As it glimmers softly,
She walks like one entranced.

With spices in her hand,
She goes to the garden tomb.

Coming from the heavy-lidded East,
The first light of day is on its way.

Surprised,
Again now,
She beholds
The open tomb.

The heavy stone
Is rolled away.

It's dark within
And she cannot see

His body.

Suddenly, two men appear.
Their clothes dazzle her:
Brilliant but
Preternatural
And terrifying.

She gasps and looks
Down to the ground.

She recalls his promise.

Why is she looking for
Him in this place?

She turns and hurries
Out into the light -

Amazed.

Nearly running into the gardener
She stops, her cheeks still wet,
And gathers herself.

He turns towards her,
Mary?

58 Closed Doors

(Jesus Comes to His Frightened Disciples)

The doors are not open into our room -
Yet here he is
Suddenly
Among us!

His gentle greeting flows for all to hear.
He stands near
And shows
His wounded hands.

He has indeed
Come
Here to us
In this place.

We hear his words
And feel his living breath.

He is present
And is risen from death.

59   Thomas

Heavy and quick steps hurry.

Up the steps he runs
And with a frantic look
Enters
Looking around quickly
Like one who fears
Pursuit.

We have seen the Lord.

Never! he sounds disturbed
And not a little angry.

All of us have seen him;
He came among us here.
He brought us his peace.

*No chance - you'll not fool me
So easily as that!
I won't
Believe unless I can see the nail holes
And put my fingers into his side.
I'll see all that first - understand?
Then I might believe you lot.*

*   *   *

Noiselessly
Jesus enters.

The doors are closed
But he is there.

He brings his peace
And gently turns his eyes
Upon his friend, Thomas:

*Here, place your finger just here
And put your hand into my side.*

I really have come, so now believe.

There is no reproof - just the truth -
And Thomas knows it is the Lord.

60 A Stranger

(An Encounter on the Road to Emmaus)

It is only the very next day -
But what a change there is in the world,
Within their wounded hearts and fractured dreams!

They are on their way;
Two's company.

It is only seven miles
But today
They trudge wearily and it seems like -
Seventy times seven.

Oh!
They had such fire and belief,
Their spirits up
With him at their head.

Now
All is so dark
And
Desolate.

Two's company
So they walk
And talk.

Out of the blue
A stranger
Saunters alongside
And listens to their words.

He does not seem to know
Any of it.

So they stop
Downcast
And tell him
The whole of
The happenings
So sad.

Lifting in mood
They speak of:
The tomb
And Mary
The vision of angels
And of John's and Peter's
Discoveries.

He calls them foolish and expounds all.
He draws them into the mystery:
The prophets
Moses
And the scriptures.

Their hearts are burning with his bright fire
But they are unsuspecting still.

Until

They stop
And are
              Breaking bread -

                            With -

                                    Jesus!

61   Fishing

(The Risen Lord Visits His Fishers-of-Men-to-be)

Simon, son of John, leads us to the boat.

It is dark but we know our work and way.
Throw the net
Circle
And heave it back in.

Drift
Further out
Throw it again.
A long night
Of toil
But we do
Not complain.

Work is good for hearts that are heavy
Like ours
And slowly the light erases.

The smell of burning charcoal
Drifts over.

Look!
We can discern a figure ashore.

His call across the lapping waves
Lifts lightly on the flowing air,
Friends, have you caught anything at all?

No, not a thing! Simon Peter responds,
Throwing down his arms with fists curled tight.

Listen boys, throw your net to the right!

Peter shrugs
He's tired
Nothing will come of it.

But we throw the net
Where the stranger said.

The water boils
With so
So many
Fish!

John
Peter's close friend
Is first to
Grasp it.

He
Whom the Lord loved
Reveals the truth:
It is the Lord.

Splash!

Simon, son of John,
Has gone
Head over
His cloak wrapped around
He wades ashore.

He hurls the boat away
Leaps in a heartbeat
To the Lord
And stops
At his wounded feet.

62   His Parting

(Jesus Ascends from Earth)

For the last forty days, often present
In person, he had been preparing them.

Now they walk back from the Mount of Olives
Full of their own personal memories.

Round and round
Again, again and again
In their minds
They can still see
His parting:

Up!

He is rising
Before their wide eyes

Up into the heavens

Above the clouds!

Going!

Gone!

Two men in dazzling white
Are there too; they amaze.

First they ask then instruct:

Men of Galilee,
With nothing to see,
Why stand so and stare?

Go as he directed you
And await his promise
Which will come upon you.
Also know that Jesus
Will return another time
Just as you saw him go.

It is only a sabbath walk from there -

A short time to absorb all of these things
Before they reach the city and its by-ways.

Soon they climb the stone steps and reach the door;
    The room seems dark and cool and very still.

63   Listen to Their Shouting
(Pentecost)

Just listen to their shouting!

Every language under the sun
Is spewing out from their mouths.

Too much of the new wine that's clear;
It's gone completely to their heads.

No!
You have the wrong angle, see?
It is not like that
Not at all.

First

The wind rises
Shakes the room
The rafters
Shutters
Everything
Until the reverberation deafens

Next

Endangering their very lives
Comes the flame.
Endangering their very lives more and more
Within the trembling darkness of the room
It burns bright and brighter
Lighting up their hearts and minds

After that

Out of the blue
Come
The words
The many voices
All clear

All can hear
The flow of language
The torrent of praise
Amazing

വ്യത്യസ്ത ഭാഷകളിൽ ഒരേ ഒരു ഓർക്കസ്ട്ര
Orchestra katika lugha tofauti sawa
Una orquesta en diferentes lenguas la misma
Оркестр на разных языках один и тот же
不同語言的管弦樂隊相同異なる言語の同じオーケストラ

'n Orkes in verskillende tale dieselfde
Një orkestër në gjuhë të ndryshme e njëjta gjë
Un'orchestra in diverse lingue la stessa
Müxtəlif dillərdə orkestr eynidir
Cerddorfa mewn gwahanol dafodau yr un fath
বিভিন্ন ভাষায় একই অর্কেস্ট্রা
ਵੱਖ-ਵੱਖ ਭਾਸ਼ਾਵਾਂ ਵਿੱਚ ਇੱਕ ਆਰਕੈਸਟਰਾ ਇੱਕੇ ਹੀ ਹੈ
Et orkester på forskellige sprog det samme
Een orkest in verschillende talen hetzelfde
Un orchestre dans différentes langues le même
Orkester erinevates keeltes sama
Isang orkestra sa iba't ibang wika na pareho
Orkesteri eri kielillä sama

भिन्नभाषासु समानं वाद्यसमूहः

ოოკესტრია სხვადასხვა ენაზე იგივე
Ein Orchester in verschiedenen Sprachen gleich
Μια ορχήστρα σε διαφορετικές γλώσσες το ίδιο
Egy zenekar különböző nyelveken ugyanaz
Hljómsveit á mismunandi tungumálum eins
Sebuah orkestra dalam bahasa yang berbeda sama
다른 언어로 같은 오케스트라
Orkestrayek bi zimanên cuda heman
Orchestra diversis linguis idem
Оркестар на различни јазици исто
Sebuah orkestra dalam pelbagai bahasa yang sama
Orkestra b'ilsna differenti l-istess
Uma orquestra em línguas diferentes a mesma
วงออร์เคสตราในภาษาต่างๆ เหมือนกัน
Farklı dillerde bir orkestra aynı
He orchestra i roto i nga reo rereke he rite tonu
Янз бүрийн хэл дээрх найрал хөгжим адилхан

विभिन्न भाषाहरूमा एउटै अर्केस्ट्रा

Et orkester på forskjellige språk det samme

Okestra nendimi dzakasiyana zvakafanana
Оркестр різними мовами однаковий
Orkiestra w różnych językach to samo
Otu egwu na asụsụ dị iche iche otu
Orchestra ni orisirisi ahọn kanna
Kungiyar makaɗa a cikin harsuna daban-daban iri ɗaya
Orchestr v různých jazycích stejný

אן אָרקעסטער אין פֿאַרשידענע לשונות די זעלבע
وركسترا بألسنة مختلفة نفس الشيء
Նվագախումբ տարբեր լեզուներով նույնը

An orchestra
In different tongues
The same

J.R. DYKES: Nicea; Heber:
Holy, Holy, Holy

Mindfulness

64 Open
(Keep life simple; try child-like love.)

It is not easy we know
To be open
Like any little child just so
Open to all

Yet this is the way we all
Must just follow
To enter through the gate
Open to all

To forgive is so hard
And forgiving
Is how we have to be
To everyone

Loving is the way to go
Open to all
Loving like a little one
To all who come

🎞 *Schutte/Hayes: Here I am Lord;*
Walla Walla University Choir

65   Riches

(We have so much. Whom might I help today? Look, plan
and act now.)

Give to everyone
Freely let it run
Your kindness and gifts
Your praises and deeds
Spreading and piling high

Generosity
Should be your hallmark
Pour out a measure
From your richest store
That runs spilling free

Lend without return
Pardon everything
Love even enemies
Turn the other cheek
Let charity flow

Listen to your heart
Feel the goodness there
Open the floodgates
See what you can do:
There. There. Yes, and there.

66   Avoid Corrupt Words

(You're a diamond; don't let your tongue say otherwise.)

Steer clear! Abstain, if you can,
From hissing hypocrisy.

My dear friend, listen to me:
Everything now that's covered
Will become open to view.
Words spoken in secrecy
Will be heard aloud by all.

Be on your guard, my dear friend,
Every hair of yours is known.
You are precious beyond price,
A hoard of infinite worth,
But accountable for yourself.

Take heed, take very great care.
By your words you may be lost
Or from them acquitted quite.
People's words flow from their hearts
And you need to see this truth.

My friend, steer clear, if you can
Of hissing hypocrisy.

67 Care

(Worried? Anxious? Why? We're in God's hands; even our length of life. Trust in Him.)

You must not worry.
There is no need see,
You have it you know
All of it is yours.
So my little one
Never be afraid.

Do not set your heart
On what is worthless.
Ravens do not sow
Nor do ravens reap,
But they have enough.
How much more for you
Are his provisions!

Never, never fret:
All in all is yours.
The flowers they show
A glimpse of his care.
His light fingers weave
Grasses of rare shape.

Not yours your life span,
He looks upon its length
With all his kindness,
So do not worry.
His great gift to you
Is his most holy
Heavenly kingdom.

68   Limited Humanity

(Offer our human frailty to God; the impossible becomes
possible.)

There he is walking on ahead
And the road is long and lonely.

For men it is impossible,
Is what he said, exactly that!

We watched the young man kneeling down,
Appealing, reaching for the key.
What must he do to find the gate
And enter eternal life?

The words are clear for all to hear.
He knows the rules given to us:
He must not kill and must not steal,
Honour his father and mother.

Easy then - he does all that,
Yes from his earliest days.
Now it comes, now comes the moment,
The long, loving look that delves deep.

Oh!

But what lies in his heart close,
Tight and safe, hidden and secure?

Like a spring then it clicks open
His love of things, of clothes and more.

The long look holds him open, wide,
While love looks in and deeply sighs.

His face falls - not so easy then
To leave all this, to leave it all.

Who can do it? Who could do it?
We all ask, appealing and reaching.

For men it is impossible,
Is what he said striding out ahead.

69   Safe Sheep

(Insecure? Feeling vulnerable?)

Those that come to me
I will keep safely
None will be cast down
I shall lose nothing
Drawn to me, sent straight,
By my Father's will

None will I turn out
But keep everyone

I give my body here
My flesh and my blood
That all may have life

Eat never to hunger
Drink never to thirst more

Live in me secure
And I will be yours -
Truly your shepherd:
Come now,
Come and be counted.

70   Be a Good Neighbour

(Help others; we're being helped.)

Take pity on the crushed
And feel for the fallen;
Do not simply pass by
Safe upon your roadway.

Stop a moment there then
To help the lost and lone;
Do not travel quickly
To your place of refuge.

Be a good neighbour now
Lend your helpful presence;
Before going forward
To finish your affairs.

You are lost and lone
In need of help for sure;
You are crushed and fallen
And look who's here for you.

71   Mary's Got It Martha!

(Worldly worries are just 'stuff.' Find God; find all.)

You worry and you fret
About the stuff of life.
So many cares and thoughts
Fill your days and nights -

But one only is all.

She chooses the right path,
So leave her be just there,
Listening and quiet.
Her choice is best you see;
You busy worker bee.

Search there and you will find;
Ask now and you will have;
Knock here and be received.

Just the one thing is all,
So find that if you can.

72   From Sorrow to Joy

(Face hardship with courage; peace and joy await.)

Her child is born into the world
And all her suffering departs:

Joy sits on her eyelids and lips,
The sharp pangs of labour are passed
And all is gurgling with smiles.

So it is with all our sorrow.
It is transient, of this earth,
And after it shines happiness,
A bliss no-one shall take from you.

You are sad now but it will pass.

In the world there are troubles;
You have to be brave and hold true.

The world is conquered,
So be strong
And you will attain lasting peace
With hearts that are shining with love.

73 Balm for Your Hurt

(Forgive all if hurt; everyone needs forgiveness.)

Go then in private
On your own
And speak with the one
Who wrongs you

Listen to each other
For peace

Where two or three
Meet together
To entreat
The spirit will come

Forgive
Forgive all
From your heart

Seventy-seven times
Is better

All are debtors
Both great and small

Forgiveness
Is the balm
Of all

74   Freedom of Choice a Great Gift
(Free will, how well do we use this gift?)

If you do this
You will get that …

Eat the apple
Gain all knowledge -
Well, did you?

Jump from up here
And be held up
On angel wings
So all will see
And follow you -
No

But giving all
Giving all
All

Freedom of choice
Out of control
Beyond reach

If you do that
You will get this ….

75   Watch over Our Hearts
(Keep a pure heart; cut bad thoughts away.)

Listen and understand
What comes out of the mouth
Comes from the heart indeed
And reveals good or bad

Watch over our own hearts
Where evil intentions spring
Murder and theft
Adultery and worse

The fruit reveals the tree
Sound fruit comes from good stock
Rotten fruit develops
From what is bad and vile

Listen

Beware of people
Fear what destroys the soul
But do not be afraid
Since we belong to God

John Hughes 1872-1914: Calon Lân; Gwyrosydd 1847-1920: Calon Lân, 'Nid wy'n gofyn bywyd moethus'

76 'Open All Hours'

(Lead a useful life; it's never too late to start.)

Work from daybreak all day
And you will receive a fair rate.
Begin at the sixth or the ninth
And you will receive your fair share.
At any hour, come and work here.

Why stand idle all the long day?
Even at the eleventh hour
There is work for you here with me,
Work for this hour and earn your due.
At any hour, come and work here.

The late comers are paid in full,
Give equal shares to all of them,
Who seemed to be lost but found work.
There's honest toil in my vineyard.
Work for my company, won't you?

The last shall be first, do you see?
Many are called but few chosen,
Yet work here is open to all
And generous rewards pour out.
At any hour, come and work here.

77   Keep My Words

(Bereaved? Mourning a loved one?)

Keep truth and keep my words

Many are the rooms now
Places for you all above
If you but keep my words

Love - love one another
Just as I have loved you
This must be your hallmark
The love you show to all

I will come back to you
You are never orphans
Because I am in you
And in my Father too

We make our home with those
Who keep my words
And peace

My own peace I give you
Love all
Keep true
Be true

This is my gift to you
A peace
The world cannot give
Peace for your soul

Peace

78 Chosen
(True friendship)

I choose you all
And call you friends

I call you friends
And share my joy

I call you friends
So bear my fruit

I call you friends
And ask your love

I call you friends
And tell you all

I call you friends
And break my bread
I call you friends

So, drink my wine

I call you friends
Stay in my love

I call you friends
Feed all my sheep

I call you friends
Keep my commands

I call you friends
So show your love

I call you friends
And give my life

79   Searching
(Mourning? Lost? Looking for meaning?)

If you lose something
You search all around
And look again just there -
Where it once rested
But you can't find it.

You will be weeping,
No longer seeing me.
You will be wailing
Because I am off,
Back to where I belong.

Do not be afraid.
I am going away
Just for your own good,
So I can send out
The spirit of truth.

If you lose something
You search more and more
And look again just there -
Where it once belonged
But cannot find it.

But

I'm not lost to you
Search for me and see.
I am here always,
With you in spirit
To the end of time.

G.F.Handel:I know that my
Redeemer Liveth, Isobel Baillie,1941

80   Heaven Thrown Open

(The stoning to death of Stephen, saint or sinner?)

Do you listen?
Do you show respect?

You are only happy
Only content
With the worthless
Things -
Man made items
And notions!

I can see heaven:

It's thrown open -
There's the Son of Man
Next to the right hand
Of the Majestic One
Everlasting in his
Perfectness.

They block their ears
At this.

Shouting
They rush
And force him out.

Furious are the stones
That they hurl.

Receive my spirit
Do not hold this
Against them

He sighs and dies.

Saul approves:
Since Stephen
Merits this end!

81   Redealt

(Even St. Paul felt like this: down, out, brought low.)

I suppose they see me like that:
A person to distrust and curse;
Someone who changed like the clouds;
A fraud, a liar, a turncoat -
Not a man to put your faith in.

It was me
After all
Going from place to place
Imprisoning
And flogging
Your true followers.

I was standing
And approving
Their stoning
Of Stephen
As well.

Now I must hurry and depart
Fly

Flee fleetly from this place.

Because they will never believe
A single word from my preaching,
I am outcast from Jerusalem.

I am being sent far away
Cast out.

No! Not
Cast out.

Cast down
And then
Redealt,
I am
To cast your light on all.

After my rank
Ignorance,
I go
To blaze
Your very truth.

82   Walking Crawling Flying
(Peter's environmental vision: care for it all.)

Walking
Crawling
Flying
Each living animal
Each bird
Every being
I see all
Yes I see

So now all is made clear
All are made clean
All saved

The vision
Reveals it
The long roll
Shows them all

Do what is right
Be just
All who are
Are all right
All are acceptable
Sure
Made pure
Pure through the Lamb

You must have heard the news
About his doing good
About his cures
His deeds
And rising
After death

Now he is shining down
Raining his grace on all
Cleansing every being
Open to everyone

He has no favourites
All are acceptable
All

All the world
He saves
Pervades all
Everything

 John Rutter: All Things Bright and Beautiful,

83 More than Enough Now

(Goodness now, goodness today, it's enough.)

Put your feet into his sandals
And worry not beyond today
Each day brings its task and burden
That's enough more than enough now

Smell with his nostrils honest truth
Simple incense rising upwards
Savour such honesty today
That's enough more than enough now

Look with his eyes just for today
See the flowers along the way
Neighbours bright with friendly faces
That's enough more than enough now

With his hands and fingers feel
Touch the lilies lightly gently
Fragile ones needing your care
That's enough more than enough now

Hear with his ears open to people
Listen to birds that sweetly sing
Open your hearts to their soft songs
That's enough more than enough now

Taste with his tongue the clean salt
Note its clear distinctiveness
The goodness in others so crisp
That's enough more than enough now

Put your feet into his sandals
And worry not beyond today
Each day brings its task and burden
That's enough more than enough now

84   Keep My Commands
(Live by the light of conscience to find peace.)

For your own good
Keep my commands

Ask and receive
Knock and enter

Keep my commands

Ask in my name
All will be yours

Keep my commands
And find my peace

Keep my commands
And live eternally

Keep
Keep
Oh keep
Your good selves true

Prayers

85   The Call of the Shepherd, Jesus

One by one he is calling -
Can you hear his voice?

There is the gate
At which he stands.
Can you see it now?

He will lead you out.
Will you follow him?

You can hear his call
As he leads the way.
Are you still behind?

Freely you may pass
In and out to pasture,
With him as your guide.

Beware the thief and wolf;
Stay safe within his flock,
Will you?

He will not run away

But stay and watch you close.
He will give his life
For you and all the rest.
Can you think of that?

He will give his life
And take it up again.

There he is at the gate,
Always waiting for you.

Join him,
If you will?

86   A Good Resolution

Make a whip of good cord
And drive away
Cruel thoughts and bad deeds
Banish them all

Sweep all the rubbish out
Dust it all off
The ego, pride and harshness
Then shine kindly

The body's a temple
For the spirit
Keep it clean and wholesome
A holy place

It is a holy place
A lovely home
A garden on the earth
For this sweet soul

87 Just Hours

Weep for the times now past
When I failed to see her hunger
And failed to notice his dry throat
Weep for the times now past

Forgive the years long gone
That I welcomed no stranger
And visited no prisoner
Forgive the years long gone

Lament for those lost days
When I left the naked
And ignored the sickly
Lament for those lost days

Give thanks for those hours past
That I gave from my heart
Riches beyond counting
Give thanks for those hours now

88 It Is Written on Our Hearts

Look with sorrow at all that's wrong:
On blindness to truth and blind alleys.
Blinding externals are nothing;
What shines within is everything.

Handsome is as handsome bethinks,
Acts, behaves and much more besides.
Riches and esteem count for naught.
Love is all: justice, mercy and more.

Pay your dues and earn your living
But do not neglect the inside;
Goodness and honesty will shine
From the flame of love in your heart.

Weep with sorrow for the wrong turns
On the way that locks out heaven.
Go back to the clear, shining road
And the loving arms that await.

89 What's Our Poison?

What's our poison?
What enthrals us?

Is it envy?
Love of yourself?
Spiteful thinking?
Perhaps it's greed
Or jealousy?

Pride is the worst
But lustfulness
Captures many
And selfishness
Runs deep in all.

Throw off my chains
Let's be washed clean.
Let's be free indeed.

Let's turn to the sun;
Oh, let my face glow.

90   Scent

The scent, it fills the house
And finds the heart, sweet nard,
Costly and fine and pure.

Anointing his feet there,
She sits, besides the jar,
Attentive as ever.

Crowds have come after him
And Martha waits on them
While her sister bends low.

91   Can I?

Learn how to refuse evil
And choose good only.
Can I, now?

Look what we do to love come down:
Dress it in purple and mock it;
Give it a reed and revile it;
Twist thorns and briars on its head.

Learn how to refuse evil
And choose good only.
Can I, now?

Forgive us all; we cannot see;
We know not what we are doing;
Look beyond our thoughts and actions;
Forgive us as only he can.

Learn how to refuse evil
And choose good only.
Can I, now?

How does he look from under the thorns?

Is it hurt or anger?

Pity?

Concern for his persecutors?
Sorrow for the perpetrators?

Learn how to refuse evil
And choose good only.
Can I, now?

How they slap and spit right at him,
Striking mocking blows on his head!

And he looks back compassionately;
Eyes them all so very sadly.

Forgiveness as only he can.

See how he does it, oh see -
And follow his way, can I?

92 If We Can

If we can

If we can
Bring back truly
Someone who has
Taken the wrong
Pathway

If we can
Bring that stray
Person back
Home

If we can
We will atone
For so much

Bring another
Back truly

If we can

93   The Wisdom of James

Never blame our temptation upon God,
For God cannot be tempted towards wrong
And God does not tempt anyone at all.

Temptation arises from our wrong desire.
It can grow within and conceive a child
Which, fully grown, gives birth in turn to death.

Wrong desires lead to wars and fighting.
We want something and we haven't got it
So we are prepared to struggle for it
And even kill if that's necessary.

We have ambition that's unfulfilled
So we fight to get our own way by force.

Ask and we will receive in abundance
But not, if what we ask is downright wrong.

Riches last no longer than flowers.
The scorching sun rises, the flower falls.

The poor,
By the world's standards only -
Mark this -
Are chosen.
Called to be rich in faith and heirs on high,
Children of God at home in his kingdom.

If we have never done a bit of good,
Never helped our neighbour in word or deed,
Can we hope to be saved?
Can we really?

Wisdom that comes down from above is pure.
It makes for sweet peace and is kind throughout.
It is full of compassion and goodness
And is considerate too, doing good.

Let's show wisdom
By living a life of humility
Sowing seeds of peace wherever we can,
If we are at all wise within.

94   What's Our Price?

Pray not to be put to the test.

Arrogant and feeble - just so -
Quick to flee
Keen to take the high ground
Your advice is sound
You know us through
Oh do not put us to the test!

Pureness of heart is hard to achieve
Washing the feet of others now
Can boost our sense of worthiness
Make us feel good in our own skins
Oh do not put us to the test!

What's our price silver or power
Esteem and greatness
Sanctity?
See ardent loving Peter fails
Oh do not put us to the test!

And do not put us to the test
For surely we will eat the fruit
Take and bite the apple dangling
Within our reach and forbidden
Oh do not put us to the test!

95　Give Honour

Give honour to God the Creator
And keep his day holy and free.

If we are to honour him well
Then, of course, we must not ever:

Kill one another wilfully
Or engage in adultery.

Nor must we ever steal or cheat
Of goods or freedom.

To corrupt innocence is worst
And lies, false witness, stop the nostril,
As they spoil all trust and belief.

Worshipping wealth and seeking fame
And the love of power
Lead to ruin.
Let's avoid their pull to perdition.

If I honour God while I live,
Caring for creation thankfully
And loving my neighbour truly,
My soul will flourish as it should.

All is given abundantly.

I may come to the water -
Though I have no money -
And drink.

Let that be;
Oh let it be.

 *Lennon McCartney: Let It Be; The
Beatles (Remastered 2009)*

Closure - but leave the door ajar

96   Get Ready … Get Set …

Escape into Egypt
Depart another way

Come out into the light
Run away from darkness

Look upon the white fields
Already the reaper comes

The hour that is to come
Is arrived even now.

Go through the narrow door
Enter whilst we can

The truth will make us free
If we will just learn it

Pray not to be tried out
Put to the test alone

Here's bread if we hunger
Here's wine for all our needs

Come to the free water
Thirsty ones come and drink

Have our lamps lit waiting
And be alert for his knock

When a great deal's given
More is then expected

Should the master come now
Would he find us wanting?

97   How Are We Using Our Freedom?

Pray not to be tested,
For we have free choices
And look how we use them.

Free choice is given to us
And the Beloved Son too.

How did we do?
Tell me.

The wind blows as it likes
But where from and where to?
Listen and we'll hear it.

Our birth comes from above.
Through water and grace
Are we born of the spirit.

Live by the truth, always.

Learn to love the light
Then we shall not be lost.

98   He Came among Us

We saw his glory:

There in the manger
Under the starlight

Teaching as a boy
Amongst the doctors

At the wedding feast
When they needed wine

On the mountain high
Truly transfigured

Feeding the thousands
On bread and two fish

In the garden - dark -
Where he prayed alone

Before the loud crowd
Calling for his death

High upon the cross
Where he forgave us

In the upper room
Appearing to all

He lived among us
In the here and now

99   Helpful Mantras - a few of many!

Better it is to be drowned in the sea
Than to destroy another person

The virtuous will shine like the sun
But destroyers will fuel the furnace

Greatness is leastness in the high kingdom
Be as a little child to gain entry

The will of the Father is obvious
Not one of the little ones should be lost

But what joy
When one that is lost is found

100 Sheep among Wolves

Sheep among wolves
Harmless as doves
But cunning still
Living on earth

Give without charge
Take no money
Come to the spring
And drink deeply

Freely give all
You have it free
So give our peace
To all we greet

Shake the dust off
Throw enmity
From our sandals
Like dirt to the ground

Do good cure all
But carry nought
Save a free hand
And friendly heart

Best live like this
Sheep among wolves
Harmless as doves
Doing God's work

101   The End of Days

Escape to the mountains
Leave the field and roof-top
From east lightning striking
Far in the west flashing
And love in most grown cold

The sun is now darkened
The moon it is dimming
And stars drooping downwards

Beat again on one's breast
And listen to the wind

Nation against nation
Not one stone left in place
No not a single stone

Increase of lawlessness
And little love around

Stay awake keep alert
Await the trumpet call
Gathering together
The birth pangs come sudden
On the clouds of heaven

The sun climbs from the north
The sun soars from the south
The sun arcs from the east
The sun there far out west
Coming - coming to all

George Harrison: Here Comes the
Sun; The Beatles (2019 Mix)

102   Trinity Trilogy

Father

Father creator
 Riding eternity at ease
Ever bringing life

Son

Son the beloved one
Our most noble saviour
And our dear brother

Spirit

Spirit of strong light
Homing sure within our hearts
With soft wings of hope

Music for the Chant for Trinity Trilogy is composed by Chris Roberts, MA, Director of Music, St Mary's Church Conwy, founder, and Director of the highly acclaimed annual Conwy Classical Music Festival.

Y Drindod

Dad, greawdwr
Farchog tragwyddoldeb rydd
Fywyd inni'n rhodd.

Fab, yr anwylaf un
Urddasol waredwr
Frawd cariadlawn cu.

Ysbryd llachar
Drig yn ein calonnau ni
Ar adenydd gobaith.

(Adaptation: A.T.H.)

Chant for Trinity Trilogy

Chris Roberts

Spi——rit of strong light, homing sure with-in our hearts,

with soft wings of hope.

Appendix   Biblical references for each piece

These references are by no means exhaustive and the reader will be able to find many more.

1   Trinity Father
    Genesis 1: 1-31; Psalms 33: 6;
    Ecclesiasticus 11 42:15-43:37; Isaiah 64:8; John
    1:3

2   Adam: 'Why Did I?'
    Genesis 3: 1-24

3   Moses, Barefoot, at the Burning Bush
    Exodus 3: 1-6

4   David a Boy Faces the Mighty Goliath
    1 Samuel 17

5   Elijah
    1 Kings 17 to 2 Kings 1:14

6   Hannah
    1 Samuel 1-2

101   The End of Days
Matthew 24: 1-31

Printed in Great Britain
by Amazon

37992509R00116